SCIENCE PROBLEMS

Things to investigate

Donald Ainley
Christopher Brown
Paul Butler
David Carrington
Graham Ellis

CAMBRIDGE UNIVERSITY PRESS

Cambridge

New York New Rochelle Melbourne Sydney

Published by the Press Syndicate of the University of Cambridge
The Pitt Building, Trumpington Street, Cambridge CB2 1RP
32 East 57th Street, New York, NY 10022, USA
10 Stamford Road, Oakleigh, Melbourne 3166, Australia

© Cambridge University Press 1987

First published 1987

Printed in Great Britain by Scotprint Ltd, Musselburgh

British Library cataloguing in publication data

Science problems: things to investigate.
  1. Science——Examinations, questions, etc.
  1. Ainley, D.
507'.6   Q182

ISBN 0 521 34825 0

Acknowledgements
The publishers would like to thank the following for supplying photographs:
Biro BiC Ltd., Rexel Ltd. and Nigel Luckhurst.

CONTENTS

Introduction 4

Why do woodlice live under stones? 6

Cooking spuds 8

Electromagnets 9

Gelatin and the bath 10

How many creepy crawlies are there in a garden? 11

Candles and oil lamps 12

How far will a ball point pen write? 14

Mouldy bread 14

The sword of Damocles 16

How much does a cup of tea cost? 17

Pencils 18

Professor Chuckabutty's liquid clock 19

Camping gas 20

Galileo's problem 21

Brine shrimps 23

Mung beans 24

Gas production by yeast 26

Which flower colours make the best indicators? 27

Steaming things 29

Growing plants from bits 30

Splashing out 32

Airy water 33

How big is the box? 34

Snails 35

Nails 36

Seagulls, pupils and crisps 37

Ice 37

Who is the forger? 38

Water, water eveywhere 39

Hints and tips section 40

INTRODUCTION

Our aim in writing these problems is to provide a resource book for use in a variety of different ways. The problems are designed to stand on their own. There is no need to follow the text in any particular order: you can dip into the book at any convenient point. We envisage the problems being used as home investigations, end-of-topic assignments in science lessons, group problem-solving exercises, science club activities, individual projects, and so on. Although initially targeted at the 11–14 age range, we feel that many of the problems have use and application for both older students and younger children.

There is much that can be done without the use of specialist equipment and we hope that the book will find as much use outside schools as it does with science teachers. There is a Hints and Tips section to which you may wish to refer before attempting some of the problems.

Teachers using the book may find, as we have, that one's own approach can make or break a problem. Discussion is an essential part of the process and the defence of a (sometimes tentative) solution in open forum can lead to improvements and more mature solutions.

These problems have not been designed with a single solution in mind. There are lines of approach (some more obvious than others) but experience has shown that it is wise to keep an open mind and welcome lateral thinking. There are very few solutions that are correct in any fixed sense of the word. Solutions should be considered in terms of their repeatability and testability. We hope you learn as much from these problems as we have, maybe returning to some again and again to attempt to find more effective solutions.

Donald Ainley   David Carrington
Christopher Brown   Graham Ellis
Paul Butler   Hull 1987

Safety

 Safety is important in all scientific work. Some of the problems have this warning symbol to show that extra caution is needed. **These problems should only be carried out under suitable supervision.**

4

APPROACHING A PROBLEM

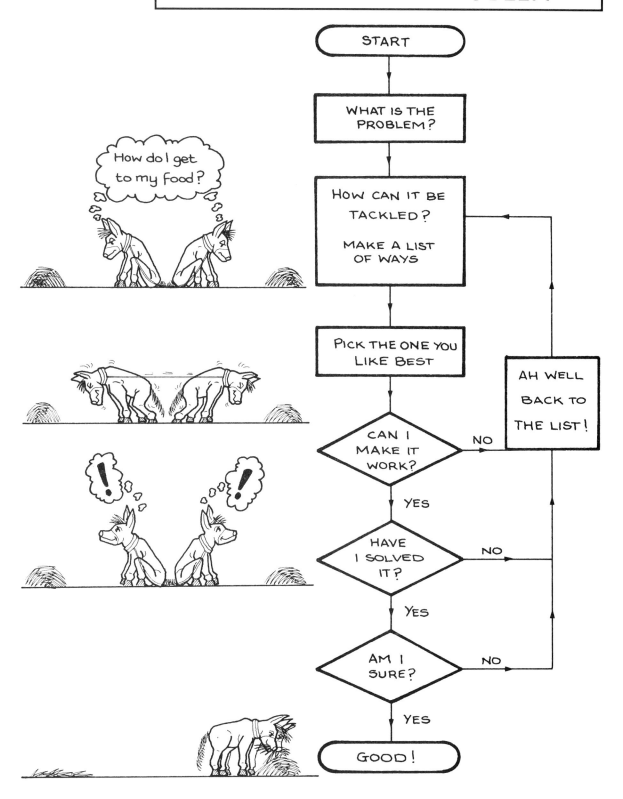

WHY DO WOODLICE LIVE UNDER STONES?

Woodlice are often found under stones or old wood. Find out if woodlice have particular preferences. For example, do woodlice prefer damp or dry conditions? Do they prefer light or dark conditions? By doing experiments with an experimental chamber you should be able to decide why woodlice live where they do.

Equipment

Some ideas for building an experimental chamber are shown in the diagram.

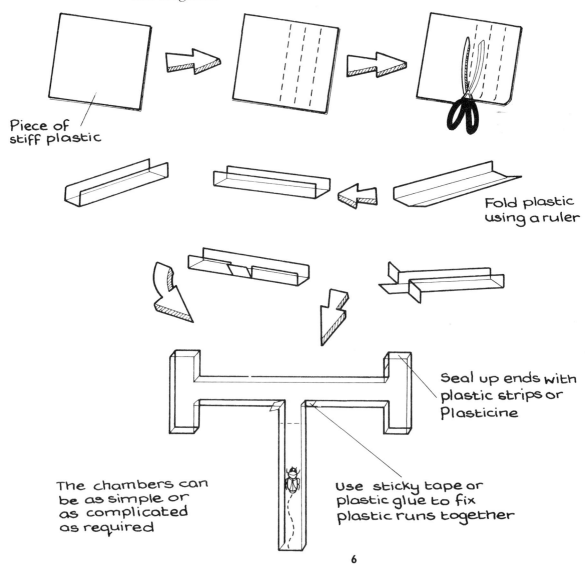

Piece of stiff plastic

Fold plastic using a ruler

Seal up ends with plastic strips or Plasticine

The chambers can be as simple or as complicated as required

Use sticky tape or plastic glue to fix plastic runs together

When planning experiments you need to consider these points.

How many woodlice should you use?
How do you decide which conditions the woodlice prefer?
How long should an experiment last?
How many choices should you test at once?
Does the time of day affect your experiments?
Are all woodlice the same?

Notes on woodlice

The woodlice for your experiments can be kept in a small aquarium or a large sandwich box. The container should have a layer of deep soil covered with dead leaves, pieces of dead wood and stones. The container should be covered but not sealed and kept in a cool dark place.

When handling woodlice take care not to damage them. They can be transferred to and from your box by brushing them gently (with a soft paint brush) from stones and dead wood into a smaller container. The woodlice can then be tipped out carefully.

When you have finished with the woodlice they should be returned to the place where you found them.

Things to try

a Different species of woodlouse.
b Different woodlice of the same species.
c Compare woodlice with different animals (e.g. snails, maggots, earthworms). Maggots can be handled in the same way as woodlice. Worms and snails can be handled directly with care.

When you have finished with the animals you have collected from the garden they should be returned to the place where you found them.

Otto le Soup, Head Chef at the local Station Hotel, is worried about his junior chefs. Some use simmering water to cook potatoes and some use vigorously boiling water. Otto wants to know which method works quicker or if there is any difference at all. If there is a quick method then Otto wants to know, so that he can get more work out of his chefs!

Solve Otto's problem using equipment from the following list

two large potatoes
peeler and knife
pan and lid
heat source
large cork
thin knitting needle
(size 12 double ended)

a range of masses
adhesive tape
water
ruler
chopping board

You need to design and make something to tell when a potato is cooked.

Other things you may want to consider

1 Do different varieties of potato cook at different speed?
2 Does the amount of water make any difference to the cooking time?

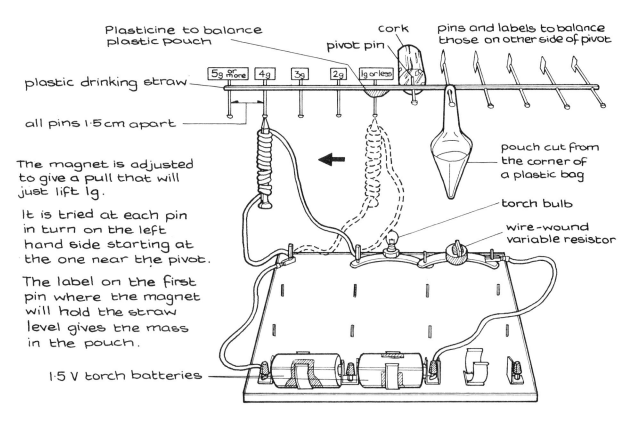

Plasticine to balance plastic pouch

cork

pivot pin

pins and labels to balance those on other side of pivot

plastic drinking straw

all pins 1.5 cm apart

5g or more | 4g | 3g | 2g | 1g or less

pouch cut from the corner of a plastic bag

torch bulb

wire-wound variable resistor

The magnet is adjusted to give a pull that will just lift 1g.

It is tried at each pin in turn on the left hand side starting at the one near the pivot.

The label on the first pin where the magnet will hold the straw level gives the mass in the pouch.

1.5 V torch batteries

Compass points north with no magnet present

Deflection increases as magnetic force gets larger

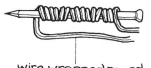

wire wrapped round

The electrical sisters Anne and Kath Ode made their own weighing machine using an electromagnet.

Problem

Can you make a better weighing machine than Anne and Kath using an electromagnet?

Things to investigate about an electromagnet

The strength of an electromagnet can be investigated like this.

1 How does the size of current flowing affect the strength of the magnet?
2 What happens to the magnet's strength if the nail is removed gradually from the coil?
3 What is the effect of altering the number of turns of wire on the coil?

GELATIN AND THE BATH

Gelatin is a powder. When mixed with water in the correct proportions it forms a solid jelly.

Instructions for mixing gelatin

1 Heat a measured volume of water, but do not let the water boil. **2** Then stir in a weighed amount of gelatin. Stir continuously until all the gelatin has dissolved. **3** Pour the liquid into a container of your choice and leave the liquid to set. The liquid can be made to set quite hard or quite soft depending how much gelatin is added to the water.

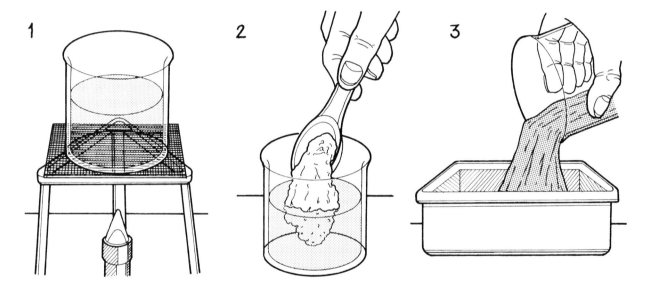

Problem

What is the smallest amount of gelatin needed to set a bath half full of water?

You must solve this problem by doing experiments with no more than three sachets of gelatin powder.

Here are a number of things to consider

You need to make a tester to see if the mixture has set.
The bath cannot be put in the fridge.
Assume that the bath is half full of water at room temperature.
How much water does the bath contain?

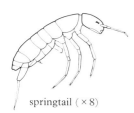

mite (× 35)

springtail (× 8)

nematode (× 25)

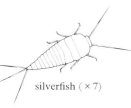

centipede (× 1½)

millipede (× 1)

silverfish (× 7)

woodlouse (× 2)

↑
These are some of the
animals you may see.

HOW MANY CREEPY CRAWLIES ARE THERE IN A GARDEN?

There are lots of small animals living in soil, which are much smaller than earthworms. These small animals can either just be seen with the naked eye or require magnification (× 10 to × 40). They can be removed from the soil by using the types of funnel arrangements shown in the diagram. In all cases the funnels can be left for one or two days. The size of sieve holes will obviously affect the size of animals collected.

Using the technique shown estimate the number of creepy crawlies in the top 15 cm of your garden soil. Is the number different for the flower border and the vegetable plot? Does the number vary with season or weather conditions?

When you have finished with the animals put them back where they came from.

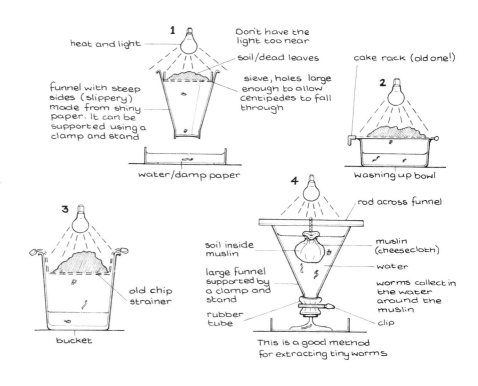

CANDLES AND OIL LAMPS

A home made oil lamp can be constructed as shown in the diagram.

1 You need: a wine cork, 5cm thin string, some cooking foil, an old beaker or jam jar.

2 Cut 4 discs from the cork. Cover one with foil and thread the string through it

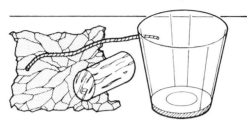

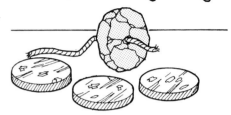

1 Cut four discs from the cork about $\frac{1}{2}$ cm thick.
2 Cover one with cooking foil and put a hole through it so that $\frac{1}{2}$ cm of string is on one side of the cork.

3 Half fill the beaker with water and pour in some cooking oil.

4 Float the cork with the string on the oil.

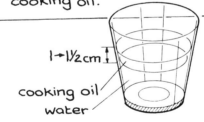

1→1½cm

cooking oil
water

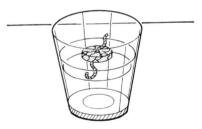

3 Half-fill the beaker with water and pour cooking oil on top to a depth of about 1.5 cm.
4 Float the cork with the string on the oil (short string at the top).
5 Use the other cork pieces (cut if required) to float around the cork with the string and keep it in the middle of the glass.

Your lamp should look like the one in the picture.

Light the wick and let there be light!

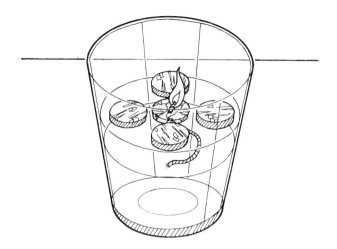

Investigating candles and oil lamps

The heat that comes from a flame can be estimated as shown in the diagram.

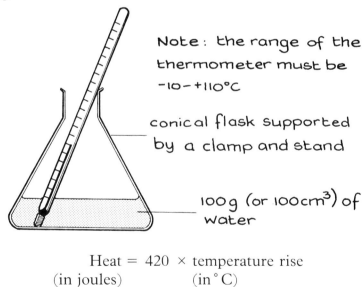

Note: the range of the thermometer must be −10 − +110°C

conical flask supported by a clamp and stand

100 g (or 100 cm³) of water

Heat = 420 × temperature rise
(in joules)   (in °C)

Problems

1 Does a candle give out as much heat as an oil lamp?
2 Does the type of oil in the lamp make any difference?
3 Which flame gives out the most light?
4 Which flame gives out the most soot?
5 Which lasts longest, 100 g of oil or 100 g of candle?

HOW FAR WILL A BALL POINT PEN WRITE?

Some of the entries in a BiC biro competition – all the models are made entirely from biro parts

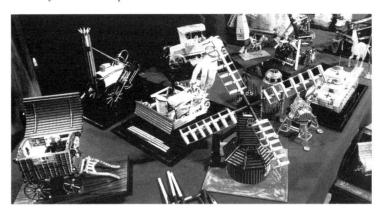

Using six sheets of paper, a ruler and a ballpoint pen with a clear plastic refill estimate how far the pen will write.

 # MOULDY BREAD

When bread is left it will eventually go mouldy.

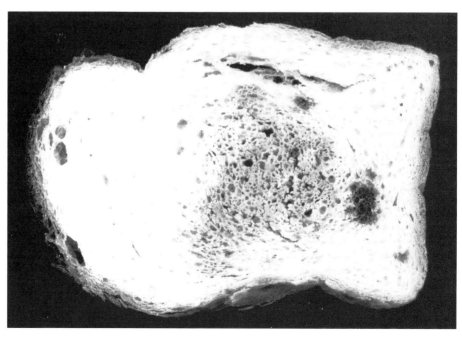

How could you slow down this process?

Consider the following

1 A method of comparing your experimental results.
2 A fair test of when the bread can be described as mouldy.
3 Type of container.
4 Temperature.
5 Moisture content of bread.
6 Type of bread.
7 Salt content of the bread.

You may find the following recipe for home made bread useful (hint: this may help with (**6**) and (**7**) above).

Recipe for home made bread

Ingredients
0.7 kg wholemeal flour, 1 teaspoon of salt, 450 cm³ lukewarm water, 15 g lard, 2 teaspoons dried yeast, 1 teaspoon sugar.

Method
Blend the sugar and yeast with 150 cm³ of the lukewarm water and leave it to froth.
Sift together the flour and salt into a bowl and rub in the lard. When the yeast is ready, add it to the flour with the rest of the water and mix to a dough.
Knead the dough on a floured surface for ten minutes then leave it to rise in a warm place for about an hour.
Knead it again for three or four minutes and split it into two one pound loaf tins. Leave the tins in a warm place (covered with a clean teatowel) until the dough has risen to the top of the tins.
Bake in a hot oven (Gas mark 8, 230°C, 450°F) for about 30 minutes. Turn the bread out of the tins and bake for a further five minutes. Leave to cool.

Further details of bread recipes can be found in standard cookery texts.

THE SWORD OF DAMOCLES

Damocles was a courtier in the ancient court of Syracuse. Legend tells that Damocles asked the ruler, Dionysius, what it was like to be in charge of things. To his surprise and horror he was invited to a banquet where he was seated under a sword that was suspended from the ceiling by a single horse hair. The idea was to give Damocles the sense of insecurity that goes with power!

Assuming that the mass of a Greek sword was between 1 and 1.5 kg, do experiments to find out if the legend could be true.

A possible source of horse hair is a violin bow (see the Hints and Tips section).

If you decide that a single hair is not enough, then make a rope of hair that would work. Estimate the number of strands needed to support at least 1 kg but no more than 1.5 kg.

HOW MUCH DOES A CUP OF TEA COST?

Titus Scrooge, great great grandson of the Dickens character had inherited his ancestor's sense of thrift. When presented with the bill in Les Jacobins, Madame Defarge's restaurant he complained about the price he was charged for a cup of tea. In the heated discussion that followed Titus insisted upon working out the cost of a single cup of tea. Madame Defarge said, 'Before you do, don't forget to take account of all the following things . . .'

1 boiling the water
2 the cost of the tea leaves
3 milk
4 sugar
5 the cost of using all the equipment (cup, saucer, kettle, etc.)

How much does a cup of tea cost?

PENCILS

Most pencils contain a core of graphite and clay wrapped in wood. The hardness of a pencil is determined by the proportion of clay and graphite that make up the core. Hard pencils contain more clay than soft pencils. Pencils are marked with a hardness scale.

The final stage in pencil manufacture – the pencils are rolled across a drum of rotating sandpaper to sharpen them

Things to investigate using pencils

How much of a pencil is used for writing, and how much is wasted in sharpening?
Which pencils wear out most quickly, soft or hard?

In comparing soft and hard pencils find out:

which leaves the most material on the paper?
which needs sharpening most frequently?
which type of lead is the strongest?

If a pencil is dropped, the core sometimes shatters inside the wooden case. This becomes noticeable when the pencil is sharpened and it keeps breaking off in little pieces.

Without sharpening it or breaking open the wood, invent a method for telling if the core is broken inside a pencil.

PROFESSOR CHUCKABUTTY'S LIQUID CLOCK

Professor Chuckabutty was working in her laboratory mixing liquids. She noticed something rather startling. She showed her experiment to her assistant Doctor Doddy . . .

Repeat Professor Chuckabutty's experiment and see what happens.

Doctor Doddy saw an immediate use for this effect. He suggested that it might be possible to get a mixture of these liquids which he could use as a timer when boiling eggs.

Do experiments to find out what would be the best mixture to use as an egg timer (Doctor Doddy likes his eggs boiled for $3\frac{1}{2}$ minutes).

CAMPING GAS

The intrepid explorer Lady Sonjia Mappe and her companion Lord Rupert Never-get-lost were planning a trip to the North Pole and beyond! They were working out what quantities of equipment they needed to take. Gas supplies for the camping stove were a problem. They could not afford to carry more than was absolutely necessary. They decided to do an experiment to see which setting on the stove used the least gas in bringing the water to the boil. They used fresh ice as the source of water and were not worried how long they had to wait for a cup of coffee.

Use a camping gas stove to find an answer to the explorers' problem.

GALILEO'S PROBLEM

When Galileo was a medical student at the University of Pisa in the sixteenth century, there was no accurate way of measuring small time intervals of the size of seconds.

Galileo knew that the speed of a patient's pulse was a useful guide to how ill they were. The problem was how to measure the pulse rate accurately. Comparing someone's pulse to that of a healthy person was not a good method because a pulse can vary considerably.

Galileo noticed the swinging lamps in the cathedral in Pisa and had the idea of a swinging weight as a timer. The swinging weight was called a **pendulum** and it became the first method of measuring small time intervals accurately. It was used as the basis of clocks for centuries.

Things to do with a pendulum

How is the swing of the pendulum affected by:

the size of the weight?
the shape of the weight?
the length of the string?
the size of the swing?

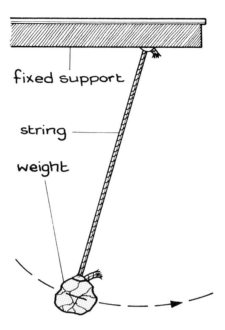

Make a pendulum that swings in time with your pulse after you have been sitting quietly. Do this without using a clock or watch. Use it to answer these questions.

What happens to your pulse rate when you run upstairs?
What happens to your pulse rate when you lie down and relax?
How long does it take for your pulse rate to return to normal after vigorous exercise?

BRINE SHRIMPS

Brine shrimps live in salt water in shallow marshes and lagoons.

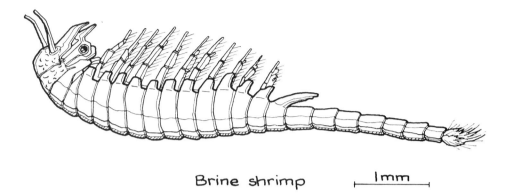

Brine shrimp |—— 1mm ——|

Their eggs can be bought in a dry state from shops specialising in the sale of tropical fish. If the eggs are placed in salt water, they soon hatch and the larvae may be seen swimming around.

When fed, they grow quickly and reach adult size (about 1 cm) in four weeks. After the experiments the live shrimps should be kept in an aquarium.

Things to find out

What are the most favourable conditions for hatching the eggs?
How quickly will brine shrimps grow?
How do brine shrimps feed?
Do brine shrimps swim at different speeds at different temperatures?
Do large brine shrimps swim faster than smaller ones?
How does a brine shrimp know which way up to swim? (They all swim on their backs!)

MUNG BEANS

Mung beans come from India. They are also grown in Australia, South-East Asia and other parts of the world. These green round beans are a good source of food. They can be cooked and eaten like other types of bean but many people like to eat mung beans when they have been made into bean sprouts.

Growing bean sprouts

Put 1 tablespoon of well rinsed mung beans into a large clean jar

Cover the top with a piece of muslin or fine meshed nylon held on with string or an elastic band

Put the jar in a warm and dark cupboard for three days...

During the three days take the jar out of the cupboard and rinse the sprouting beans well in fresh cold water drain them and return them to the cupboard. Do this about three times a day.

If you are going to eat the sprouts, tip them out of the jar when they are ready and rinse them well in cold water to clean them and remove the seed coats. They will keep in the fridge for a few days.

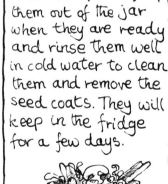

BEANSPROUT, MUSHROOM and CELERY SALAD

SERVES 4

1 large head celery.
8oz (225g) bean sprouts.
6oz (175g) button mushrooms.
3 tablespoons olive oil.
1 teaspoon soy sauce.
½ teaspoon dry mustard.
½ teaspoon sugar.
1 tablespoon wine vinegar.
Salt and ground black pepper.

Slice the celery. Rinse the bean sprouts and add them to the celery. Wash and slice the mushrooms, then add them to the other vegetables. Make a dressing by mixing together the oil, soy sauce, mustard, sugar, wine vinegar and salt and pepper. Pour the dressing over the vegetables and turn them so they are all coated with it.

The sprouts are nice in salads. They will keep in a fridge for a few days. The sprouts can also be cooked.

When mung beans are made into sprouts they increase in mass about three times. Their volume increases by much more than this. You will need to find a way of measuring how much water stays in the jar when the beans are rinsed to solve these problems.

Does the gain in mass of the beans equal the mass of water that stayed in the jar?

Does the gain in volume of the beans equal the volume of water that stayed in the jar?

GAS PRODUCTION BY YEAST

Yeast is a microscopic living thing which needs sugar to live. It uses sugar and makes a gas called **carbon dioxide**. We make use of the gas production in bread-making. The gas makes the dough rise so that the bread becomes light and spongy when it is baked. At home we can use either fresh or dried yeast for baking.

Making yeast produce gas

What you need

a packet of dried baker's yeast
a small amount of fresh baker's yeast
granulated white sugar

a coffee jar
an eye-dropper
a small piece of plasticine

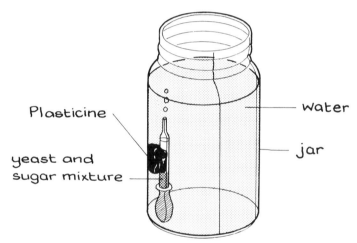

Getting started

Dissolve some sugar in the water, add yeast and stir well. Suck up some of the mixture into the eye-dropper. Use the plasticine to stick the eye-dropper to the inside of the jar. Add some warm water so that the tip of the eye-dropper is well below the surface of the water. Bubbles of gas which are formed in the mixture will escape from the tip of the eye-dropper and can be counted.

Find out if the bubbling is changed by:

1 Altering the temperature of the water in the jar.
2 Making the sugar solution stronger.
3 Giving the yeast grape sugar (glucose) instead of cane sugar (sucrose).
4 Using different yeast, for example, brewer's yeast.

WHICH FLOWER COLOURS MAKE THE BEST INDICATORS?

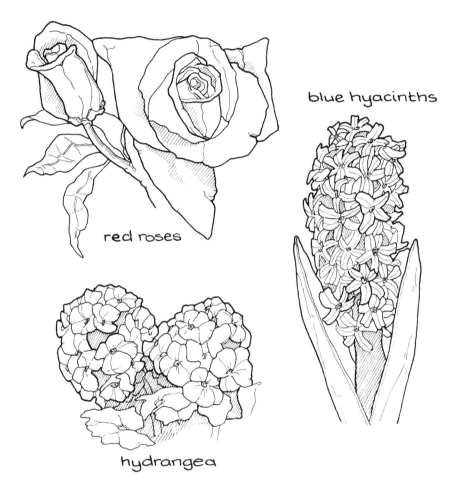

red roses

blue hyacinths

hydrangea

Acids can be recognised by adding an indicator. An indicator is a coloured solution which turns a different colour when an acid is added to it. The first indicators to be used came from plants. You can use red cabbage juice as an indicator. In many plants there are colours in the petals. Can petal colours be used as indicators?

How to get started

Indicator solutions are usually quite deep in colour. You get the best results by starting with deeply coloured flowers such as red or purple geraniums, red roses, purple crocuses, blue hyacinths, blue speedwell and red wallflowers.

The colour can be extracted from the petals by grinding them with methylated spirits. You can use either a pestle and mortar, or a plastic spoon in a yoghurt pot, or a glass rod in a beaker. Try to make a solution which is as deeply coloured as possible. The petals can either be filtered off, or the coloured solution can be poured off the petals. If you are doing this experiment at home, you could use citric acid (from a Pharmacy or Home Brew shop) or vinegar as acids, and garden lime as an alkali. Dissolve the citric acid or garden lime in water before use.

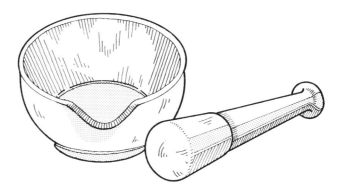

pestle and mortar

Some questions that you may be able to answer in this problem

1 How can the coloured substances be extracted from flower petals?
2 Do all petal colours act as indicators?
3 Does it matter how much acid is added?
4 Do different acids act in different ways with the indicator?
5 Will an alkali change the colour of the indicator?
6 Does it matter how much alkali or what sort is used?
7 In what way do all petal colours seem to act the same in this investigation?
8 Can you make indicator paper from petal colour, just as we have litmus paper? If so how could you do it?
9 Which flower petals seem to make the best indicators, and why is this so?

STEAMING THINGS

Granny Smith makes her Christmas puddings using a very old recipe

The puddings are *DELICIOUS* but they have to be cooked for a very long time...

The recipe says the puddings have to be steamed for FIVE HOURS...

Steaming means heating the pudding in the steam above a pan of simmering water

Problem

Granny Smith had bought a new pan and steamers (used for cooking vegetables or puddings in steam). The pan holds 1000 g of water. She wants to know how long she can leave the pan of water simmering before the 1000 g of water boils away. Can you find an answer for her?

Things you could use

beaker (250 cm³), weighing scales, Bunsen burner, tripod, wire gauze, clock or stopwatch, graph paper, water (250 g only).

Things to remember

1 You can only have 250 g of water.
2 You must not boil away more than 200 g of water.
3 A Bunsen burner full on will provide enough heat to make Granny Smith's pan of water simmer.

GROWING PLANTS FROM BITS

Gardeners are very careful when they are weeding their vegetable patches to dig up entire weed plants rather than leaving bits behind in the soil. They do this because many plants can grow again from any bits that are left. Some plants can grow again from any bits that are left. Some plants can grow from bits of leaf, stem, or root, others from one part only and yet others not at all.

Things to find out

Which common weeds can grow from bits of stem, root and leaf? What is the smallest part of a plant that a new plant can grow from?
Do new plants grow from bits whichever way up they are positioned? (Try upside down leaf bits and wrong-way-up stems and root bits).
How long does it take a new plant to grow from a bit?
Does growth from a bit depend on
a how wet the soil is,
b how much light is available, or
c how warm it is?

Hints

Try growing the bits in small flower pots filled either with fine (e.g. sieved) garden soil or potting compost. The soil or compost should be moist but not too wet. After putting the bits into the pots, place each pot in a separate polythene bag and tie the top of it. Bits of leaf should be placed on the surface of the soil, other bits buried in it.

Here are some plants you might try.

Dandelion

Cow Parsley

Daisy

Bindweed

Thistle

Dock

Couch
Grass

Nettle

SPLASHING OUT

Labels on pots of paint usually give some idea of what surface area the paint will cover. This could be misleading because it might depend upon the type of surface the paint is used on.

It is possible to buy sample pots of emulsion paint for use as colour testers. Use these to find answers to the following problems.

1 Using as little paint and paper as possible, make estimates of the area the paint will cover if it is used on the following papers:
   a anaglypta
   b superglypta
   c woodchip
   d lining

2 Use the small pot of paint to estimate how much paint is needed to paint a room in your house. (Check your result next time you decorate).

AIRY WATER

If a beaker of water is filled from a fast-running tap and left to stand for several hours, bubbles of air can be seen in the water.

A method of collecting the air from water is shown in the diagram.

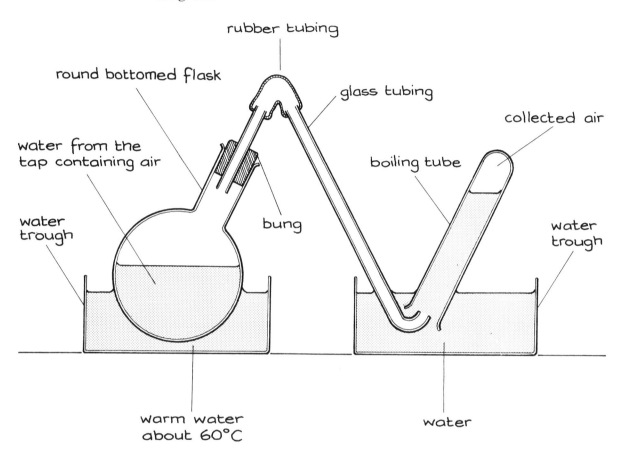

Things to find out

1 Find out how the number of degrees the tap turns affects the volume of water per second that comes from it.

2 Does the water flow from the tap affect the amount of air in the water?

3 What happens to the volume of water when the air comes out of it?

4 Does water from the hot tap contain the same amount of air as water from the cold tap? (**Note:** you need a fair way of comparing water from the two taps. The only difference should be their temperature.)

HOW BIG IS THE BOX?

An open topped box can be made out of a sheet of card and some sticky tape as shown in the diagram.

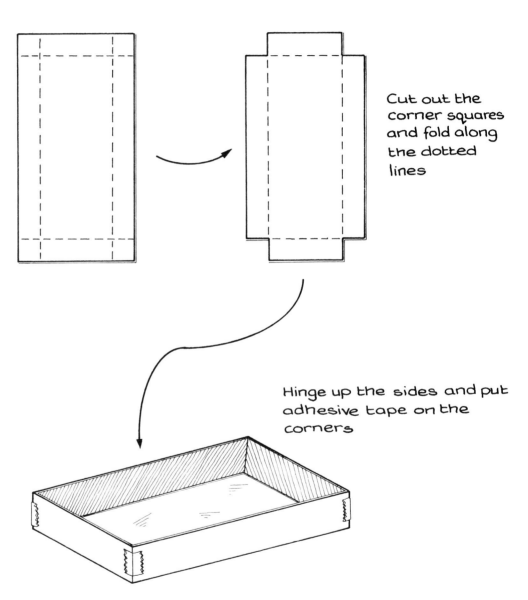

Mark the card with dotted lines so that there is an identical square at each corner

Cut out the corner squares and fold along the dotted lines

Hinge up the sides and put adhesive tape on the corners

If the box is then lined with cling film it will hold water.

What size of square must be cut from the corners of a piece of A4 card (297 mm × 210 mm) to make a box with the maximum possible volume?

SNAILS

You can collect several different sorts of snails from a garden or the park. They can be kept for a long time in 'snaileries' like the one shown in the picture.

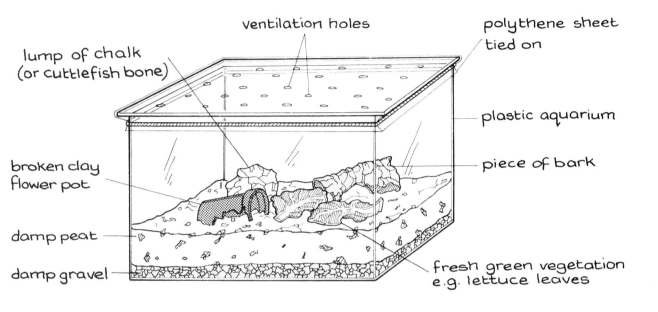

Start this problem by collecting a few snails of the same kind and set up a 'snailery'.

Have a good look at a snail. If it doesn't want to co-operate, place it in a dish of warm shallow water to coax it out of its shell. (Don't worry it will not drown!)

Questions

1 What do snails eat?
2 How much do they eat in a day?
3 How do they eat?
4 When do they move around most?
5 Why do they make slime?
6 Do they always make the same amount of slime?
7 How quickly can snails move?
8 Does the surface affect the speed at which snails move?
9 Can snails see, smell, feel and taste? (If so, what?)
10 How does a snail breathe?
11 How strong is a snail? (How much can a snail pull?)

Things to do with snails outside

Find out where snails live in the garden or park. You can mark some with small drops of quick-drying paint on the **underside** of the shell. This allows you to recognise the snail again. Try to find out if snails behave like homing pigeons!

When you have finished all your work with snails they should be returned to the garden or park where you found them.

NAILS

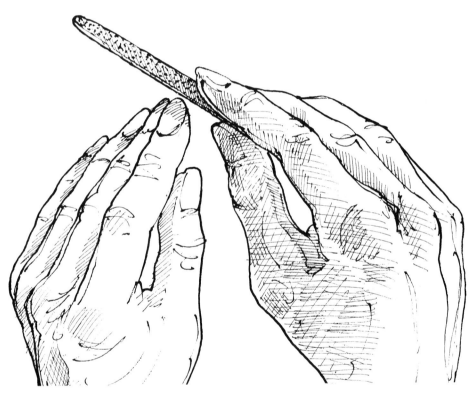

1 Do **all** your finger nails grow at the same speed?
2 Do finger nails grow faster than toe nails?
3 Do your nails grow faster in the summer than in the winter?
4 Do the nails of young people grow faster than those of adults?

Work out a way of measuring accurately the growth of a finger nail over a certain length of time. You may have to persuade some people that this is all in the cause of science!

When you have found a good way of measuring nail growth use it to answer these questions.

SEAGULLS, PUPILS AND CRISPS

Nearly everybody likes crisps (potato chips) and many children eat them in the playground. Scraps of crisps (potato chips) can be left over and in the winter seagulls seem to enjoy these.

But

How do they know the crisps (potato chips) are there in the first place? (Has it got something to do with the presence of large numbers of noisy pupils?)
Do the seagulls only visit at certain times of the day?
Do they prefer any particular flavour of crisp (potato chip), such as salt and vinegar, etc.?
Will they go away if crisps are no longer eaten in school?
Will they eat other things besides crisps (potato chips)?

Find out!
If your school doesn't have any seagulls see what you can do at school or at home with sparrows or starlings.

ICE

On a hot day you can cool down your drink of coke or orange juice by adding ice cubes. A popular adult drink in the United States is 'Scotch on the rocks' in which ice cubes have been added to whisky.

Problems

1 Does the ice melt at the same speed in all drinks?
2 Are all drinks cooled by the same amount when ice is added?

What you will need

a solution of sugar in water (instead of coke) and a solution of citric acid in water (instead of lemonade or orange juice)
a solution of alcohol in water
   (instead of whisky)   beakers
ice cubes   a thermometer
a measuring cylinder   a stopclock

What you will have to decide

1 How will you make sure the 'drinks' are all at the same temperature at the start?
2 How will you measure the amount of ice used?
3 How will you measure how fast the ice is melting?

WHO IS THE FORGER?

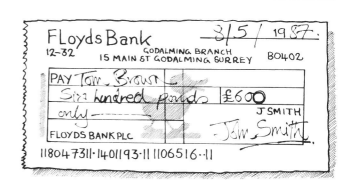

John Smith had sent a cheque for six pounds, written in black ink, to Tom Brown. When his bank statement arrived, John found that Tom had been paid six hundred pounds. When the bank manager showed him the cheque, John saw that the word 'hundred' and two noughts had been added to it, also in black ink.

Both Tom and his wife have black pens but they are of different makes. The bank cashier, who is Tom's brother, also has a black pen of another sort.

You are given the black pens of John Smith, Tom Brown, Tom's wife and the bank cashier and the cheque. Find out if the cheque has been forged and, if it has been forged, who added the extra words and figures.

Getting started

You will need to know that:

1 the makers of ink for ball pens mix up a number of colours to make black.

2 different coloured inks can be separated by **chromatography**.

Some questions you may be able to answer in this investigation

1 Do all the makers of black pens use the same colours for their inks?

2 Was the word 'hundred' written in a different ink from the word 'six'?

3 Whose pen could have been used to forge the cheque?

4 Which colours in inks seem to be absorbed into the paper best?

5 Which liquid seems to dissolve the inks best?

WATER, WATER EVERYWHERE

Baron Hardup has set up business with his daughter Cinderella and son-in-law Prince Charming. There is a natural spring in the grounds of Hardup Castle. The Baron makes Cinders fill bottles with spring water, he labels them 'Healthy Natural Spring Water' and the Prince persuades the local supermarket to sell them at a vast profit.

The spring only runs slowly and no matter how hard Cinders works there is a limit to how many bottles she can fill in a week. The Castle is near the sea and several rivers and streams flow through the estate. There is also a garden tap for a hosepipe and a large water-butt full of rainwater near the Castle Greenhouse. The Baron wonders about filling bottles with water that is not spring water. This would increase their production and profit but he needs to know if anyone could tell the difference.

How can he decide if samples of all the different types of water are the same?

Things that he (and you) might try

1 looking at samples of water under a microscope
2 filtering them
3 evaporating them
4 finding their electrical conductivity (how much electricity they let through). Ask your teacher to arrange the electricity supply.
5 adding soap solution, a small portion at a time, and shaking
6 adding a small volume of potassium permanganate [potassium manganate(VII)] solution
7 measuring pH

The Baron could carry out these (and other) tests on freshly-collected water samples and also on samples of each of the waters which have been boiled and allowed to cool. He should remember that he is comparing the water samples and therefore should carry out fair tests.

HINTS AND TIPS SECTION

This section gives outline details of what we feel is the most obvious approach to some of the problems. Specific details are provided where we feel that this is essential. Experience of using problems in a teaching situation has shown that there are seldom unique solutions in terms of method and in some cases there are a variety of possible outcomes. When using problems in a teaching situation we have selected teams by drawing lots (regardless of ability) and awarded a small prize on the basis of team work, method and result. To do this we have used problems both as written out here and in an adapted form to suit our own constraints of equipment and time. Some sort of presentation where solutions are put to the test adds greatly to the exercise. It is hard to convey the sense of positive feedback we have experienced in using problem solving as a teaching method. Suffice to say that the sense of enthusiasm shown by both pupils and staff is far beyond anything we imagined it may be and out of all proportion to the small prize that may be offered!

Please use these hints and tips as a guide and not a set of solutions.
Do not be afraid to adapt a problem to meet your own circumstances.

THE USUAL GUIDELINES FOR SAFETY IN SCHOOL SCIENCE SHOULD BE FOLLOWED WHEN USING THIS BOOK. (See 'Safey in Science Laboratories' published by HMSO, third edition 1978.)

Hints for 'Why do woodlice live under stones?'

Materials useful for making choice chambers include stiff plastic sheets, margarine tubs, yoghurt pots, sticky tape and Plasticine. There are several varieties of woodlice. Some common ones are shown below. Woodlice will need a settling time before each experiment.

Snails and earthworms can be found in gardens, parks, and hedgerows. Maggots can be obtained from fishing tackle shops.

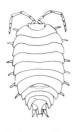
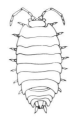
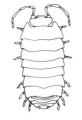
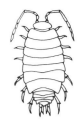

Oniscus asellus
up to 15 mm

Porcellio scaber
up to 17 mm

Armadillidium vulgare
up to 18 mm

Philoscia muscorum
up to 10 mm

Hints for 'Cooking spuds'

Safety point: be careful with the hot water.

The potato tester should give results that are independent of the operator. To be fair, test experiments should be done using the same variety of potato, except when the differences between varieties are being tested.

Hints for 'Electromagnets'

Safety point: be careful with electricity.

It is intended that the problem should be tackled at school where there is access to circuit board apparatus and an accurate balance (± 0.5 g).

The balance shown should be made so that the straw swings freely on the pivot pin. It can be made of a longer straw and the number of pins increased accordingly. If the nail or pin need demagnetizing first, this can be done using a coil connected to a low voltage a.c. power supply and slowly withdrawing the pins/nail from it. For example, a 250 turn coil connected to 12 V a.c. can be used with a suitable series rheostat (e.g. 11 Ω 4 A) and meter to limit the current to 3 A. Note that such a coil should only be turned on for short periods of up to 30 seconds to prevent it getting hot.)

The torch bulb and wire wound resistor (25 Ω) are standard circuit board equipment. The nail should be made of soft iron, and with the apparatus as shown, about 200 turns of wire are needed. The strength of the magnet can be varied by adjusting the resistor or changing the number of turns. The brightness of the bulb gives a crude indication of current. An ammeter (0–1 A) can be used in the circuit.

A different type of balance can be based on the Worcester Current Balance (see Nuffield Physics Guide to Experiments II, Longman/Penguin 1967). Details of circuit board experiments are widely available in school textbooks.

Hints for 'Gelatin and the bath'

Safety points: be careful with the hot water.

A gelatin tester can be made by using a fixed mass on a fixed area and seeing if the surface will support this without breaking. The gelatin and water mixture should be allowed to reach room temperature before testing. A kitchen measuring jug would be a suitable container.

Hints for 'How many creepy crawlies are there in your garden?'

Magnification of $\times 10$ can be obtained with a hand lens or magnifying glass. Higher magnification will need some sort of microscope.

To keep the soil animals alive collect them in a high-sided dish with a thin layer of plaster of Paris and charcoal paste set on the bottom. (RECIPE: use 4 teaspoons plaster of Paris, $\frac{1}{2}$ teaspoon charcoal powder and water to mix to a smooth paste. Pour and leave to set.) Springtails, bristletails and some worms can be fed with moist yeast. Many other animals are carnivores.

Hints for 'Candles and oil lamps'

Safety points: be careful with flammable liquids and naked flames—a heavy damp (*not* dripping) cloth should be available to smother the oil lamp if it catches fire.

Wine bottle corks can be obtained from home-brewing shops. Vegetable oil is a suitable oil to use. For different types, sunflower, soya or mixed vegetable oil can be used. Investigation **4** requires an accurate balance ($\pm 0.01\,\text{g}$) if mass is used as the basis of measurement. A light meter in a camera can be used for both **3** and **4**. Large mass changes in **5** will require long experiments.

Hints for 'How far will a ball point pen write'

An accurate balance ($\pm 0.01\,\text{g}$) is needed if mass is used as the basis of measurement.

Hints for 'Mouldy bread'

Safety point: make sure that you dispose of the bread at the first sign of mould. Disinfect containers after use, or use disposable plastic bags.

Keep the bread away from other foodstuffs and in a covered container. It should be inspected every day.

Hints for 'The sword of Damocles'

Horse hair is expensive and variable in strength. Possible substitutes are tacking cotton and fine fishing line.

Hints for 'How much does a cup of tea cost?'

Safety point: be careful with hot water.

Accurate weighing may be required. Current prices for ingredients, kitchen equipment, gas/electricity and an estimate of the lifespan of utensils, teacups, etc. are needed.

Hints for 'Pencils'

Accurate weighing is one way of testing which type of pencil leaves the most lead on the page. One method of determining if a lead is broken is to investigate its electrical resistance. Leads sold for clutch pencils and technical drawing (propelling pencils) may be useful.

Hints for 'The liquid clock'

Safety point: be careful with the chemicals; this problem should be done in a school.

The solutions mentioned in the text are as follows:

A = 0.5 M potassium iodide (83 g of potassium iodide in water to make 1000 cm³ of solution).
B = 0.01 M sodium thiosulphate (2.48 g of sodium thiosulphate in water to make 1000 cm³ of solution).
C = 2% Starch solution (2 g of starch in 100 cm³ of water, brought to boiling then cooled).
D = Saturated solution of potassium peroxodisulphate (VI) (potassium persulphate) in water ($K_2S_2O_8$).
E = water.

The solutions **must** be mixed in the order given in the text.

Hints for 'Camping gas'

Safety point: be careful with hot water and naked flames; ensure adequate ventilation.

Accurate weighing may be required (to $\pm 0.1\,g$).

Hints for 'Galileo's problem'

The number of seconds for a pendulum to execute a complete swing (i.e. there and back) provided that the angle of the swing is small (10° or less) is given by:

$$T = 2\pi\sqrt{(\text{length of pendulum in metres} \div 9.81)}$$

Hints for 'Brine shrimps'

Hatching instructions are given on the side of the container in which the eggs are sold. Although aeration is not vital it does produce higher survival rates. If this is not possible the container in which they are cultured should have a wide mouth or, better still, use a plastic aquarium. A hand lens or magnifier should be used to look for newly-hatched larvae. These should be fed (sparingly) on a suspension of baker's yeast which is added to the water in sufficiently small volumes so that the water does not cloud unduly. As the animals grow bigger they can be fed on ground-up, flaked, fish food suitable for tropical or cold-water fish.

The eggs hatch over a wide temperature range but if a reasonably constant temperature of 22–24°C can be maintained, e.g. by using an aquarium heater, hatching occurs within 24 to 48 hours. A low-power microscope is an advantage for making observations on the smallest larvae and particularly useful to investigate feeding. If a large specimen is placed on a microscope slide, entangled in a few threads of cotton wool and supplied with particles of fish food, the use of the limbs in feeding and the appearance of food in the gut can be observed.

Investigations on swimming speed are best carried out in glass or clear plastic tubes.

Orientation of the animal in the water is with respect to the direction of the light, its ventral (back) surface is maintained at right angles to this.

Hints for 'Gas production by yeast'

The following mixture produces rapid bubbling at a temperature of about 25°C: 8 g fresh bakers' yeast (or 4 g dried active yeast)

10 g sugar
100 cm³ water

The mixture should be stirred thoroughly before being sucked up into the eye-dropper. Glucose and sucrose can be obtained from a chemist's shop.

Hints for 'Which flower colours make the best indicators?'

The colours from deeply-coloured flowers can easily be extracted with ethanol, either in the form of industrial methylated spirits or of domestic methylated spirits. The purple dye in the latter has no effect on the colour change in the solution when acid or alkali is added. The colour of the solution in ethanol may soon fade but this does not prevent the extract acting as an indicator.

Generally whatever the colour of the flower, the extract turns red when acid is added and green on the addition of a weak alkali such as lime water or sodium hydrogencarbonate (baking soda). The use of sodium hydroxide solution should be avoided since it is likely to precipitate the colouring matter, leaving a yellow solution. The extracts of certain species of flowers (e.g. some yellow roses) do not show the general colour changes, and the purple crocus yields an extract which will act as a universal indicator.

Safety points: be careful with flammable liquids, ensure adequate ventilation.

Hints for 'Steaming things'

Safety point: be careful with hot water.

Hints for 'Splashing out'

One method involves the use of an accurate balance (± 0.01 g) if mass is used as the basis of measurement. The different types of paper mentioned in the experiment can be obtained from a hardware shop.

Hints for 'Airy water'

A fair comparison between taps can be based on rate of flow measured as either mass per second or volume per second. For both measurements a quantity of water should be collected over a reasonable time span (30 seconds or so, depending on the speed of the tap) and an average value per second calculated.

Hints for 'How big is the box'

The value of x can be estimated by plotting volume against x.
x = height of the box.

Hints for 'Snails'

Safety point: be careful when using 'superglue' in the experiment to test pulling ability, it is very strong and can bond fingers together.

The snails can be fed on lettuce or cabbage leaves. Food preferences can be investigated by placing snails (starved for two or three days) in plastic containers in which there are several different sorts of leaves. Try mint, holly, rhubarb and nettles as well as their 'normal' food. The mass of material consumed can be estimated by tracing the nibbled leaf onto squared paper. The action of their file-like feeding structure (radula) can be seen by observing them dealing with dried films of flour or yeast stuck on to a glass sheet. The glass can be turned over when the snail is feeding and the process observed using a hand lens.

Substances such as vinegar and dilute ammonia solution can be placed as a ring around a snail on a glass plate. If the snail's foot is sensitive to the chemical the animal will not cross the circle. Clearly it is necessary to compare the behaviour with what happens when a ring of water is used.

Smell and taste are tested using small lumps of cotton wool held in forceps, or small paint brushes, dipped in test liquids.

A breathing hole can be located on the snail's right hand side just below the rim of the shell. The length of time the hole is open varies and can be investigated.

A suitable arrangement for investigating pulling ability is shown in the diagram.

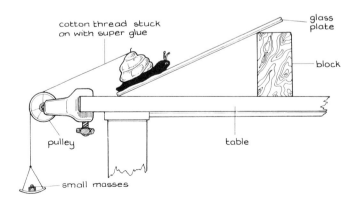

46

Hints for 'Ice'

For a fair test the drinks should all be at the same starting temperature, and the ice cubes should all be of the same dimensions and at the same temperature.

Safety point: do not consume experimental liquids.

The rate of melting of the ice can be measured by taking out the ice cube at intervals and quickly measuring it, or by measuring the rise in surface level (compared to the level before the ice was put in) when the ice cube is removed.

Citric acid can be obtained from a pharmacy or home brew shop.

Hints for 'Who is the forger?'

Safety point: be careful with flammable liquids and chemicals; ensure adequate ventilation.

It is intended that this problem should be set out by a teacher for a group of pupils.

The inks on two portions of the 'cheque' will be compared chromatographically with the inks in the ballpens under test. The cheque should be cut into strips through the portions which appear to have been added and through those portions which are known to be original (e.g. the date). For a separation adequate for comparison of the inks, it may be necessary to supply an enlarged version of the cheque, or a version with an appreciable margin, so that the strips can be of reasonable length. Chromatograms of the inks from the ballpens of the 'suspects' should be prepared on the same paper as the cheque. It will depend upon the teacher's inclination as to whether a crime has been committed and, if so, who is the culprit. The most appropriate method of separation in this investigation would involve vertical elution, although it might be possible to use the 'wick' method or to add solvent dropwise to the writing by means of a fine test pipette.

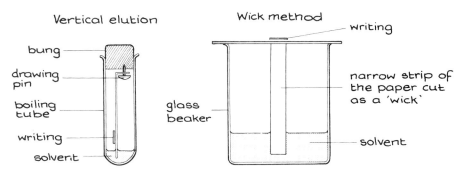

The most suitable solvent for separating the inks is likely to be a mixture of butan-1-ol (60 cm³), ethanol (20 cm³) and 2 M aqueous ammonia (20 cm³). Propanone or ethanol can be used and will probably give acceptable results.

Hints for 'Water, water everywhere'

Safely points: be careful with hot water and chemicals. **N.B.** Mains voltage can be fatal. Do **not** build a circuit using a mains transformer without reference to a suitably qualified person to check safety.

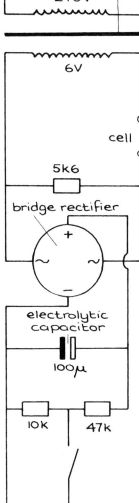

The most interesting results are to be obtained by selecting samples of widely differing composition (e.g. sea water, distilled water, water collected in a chalk or limestone area, and fresh water collected in a soft water area).

Microscopic examination is only likely to give useful results if the water samples are freshly collected. Filtration, evaporation, and measurement of pH will probably fail to show significant differences between the samples, whatever the source. Potassium manganate(VII) solution can be used to detect the presence of organic material (living organisms, micro-organisms, waste products from living things, etc.). A suitable concentration is about 0.01 M (approx. 0.16 g in a litre of distilled water). The purple colour is removed at different rates depending upon the amount of organic material present. Calcium salts can be detected by using soap solution. The amount of soap solution needed to form a lather increases as the amount of calcium salt present increases. It may be necessary to adjust the concentration of potassium manganate(VII) and soap solution depending on the water sample. The electrical conductivity can be measured with a low voltage a.c. supply. This indicates differences in the presence of non-organic material (e.g. dissolved salts). The following arrangement has indicated significant differences between natural water samples:

The cell consists of two short lengths of stainless steel tubing mounted 2 cm apart in a small block of wood. The output of the device can be connected to a d.c. voltmeter or to the analogue port of the BBC microcomputer. The voltage drop across the 5.6 K resistor is a measure of the current flowing through the cell, and hence the conductivity of the water.